AF244967

A Little Feral

Poems by Maria Giesbrecht

Write Bloody Publishing
America's Independent Poetry Press

Los Angeles, CA

writebloody.com

First edition.

ISBN: 9781949342819

Cover Design by Derrick C. Brown

Edited by Haley Hutchinson

Proofread by Ronnie K. Stephens

Author Photo by David Casco

Typeset in EB Garamond.

Printed in the USA

Write Bloody Publishing Los Angeles, CA

Support Independent Presses writebloody.com

A Little Feral

MARIA GIESBRECHT

ADDITIONAL PRAISE

"Maria's collection of poems is amazingly vulnerable in a way that will deeply impact any reader. She captures pain and beauty in such a way that I found myself wanting to commit to memory so many lines and paragraphs in her poems. It's truly a book I will not forget." - Hannah Rosenberg, USA Today bestselling author of *Same*

"Maria Giesbrecht is a mesmerizing storyteller, she weaves words with gentle intensity. The poems here fill a silence that has long surfaced between people and places. The poems will provoke you to revisit your own experiences, finding both the hurt and light in them." -Theresa Lola, author of *Ceremony for the Nameless*

"Giesbrecht rips open the seams of a childhood under the thumb of a controlling father and church, and then invites the reader to watch as she slowly stitches a more tender life in its place. When force meets forgiveness and freedom, the result is a little feral." -Sarah Hanson, author of *Conjuring the Hurricane*

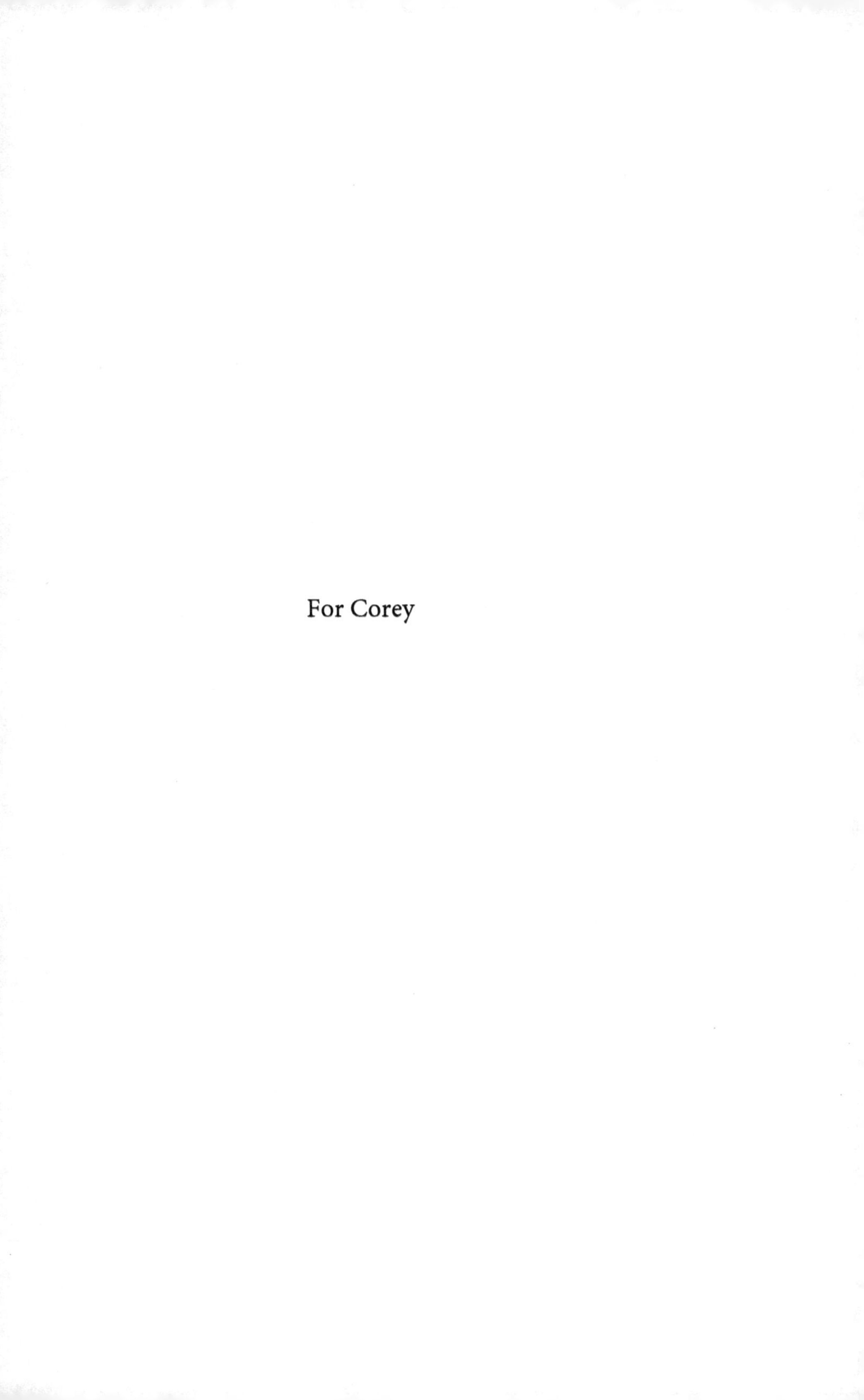

For Corey

TABLE OF CONTENTS

A LITTLE FERAL

There's a car in my neighborhood with the bumper sticker
a little feral and I think of how yesterday I sawed off
two slices of watermelon and let them drip disgusting
down my elbows. I catch myself sometimes. I forget
to sweep the corners on purpose or run a load of laundry
without soap. I press into the world's chest — will it budge?
I didn't know I loved my first boyfriend until I yelled *fuck
you* one night and he didn't leave. I do this — I push
back like a palm in church. I didn't know I loved God
until he grated the black night into my bowl and didn't flinch
when I threw up a few stars.

"Everything has two endings — a horse, a piece of string, a phone call."

—*Jane Hirshfield*

MY FATHER, A HORSE WHISPERER

It wasn't cloudy   or raining
the day   he hit me   I was tired
of hearing   mariachi music   in the mornings
I'm saying   there was a perfect   motive
I turned   the radio off   with a firm yank
of it   I'm saying   I was high
on teenage power   when he grabbed
the wire   twisted the end   between fingers
and   whipped my soft cheeks   like a slow horse
I'm saying   I didn't hate it   I felt alive
        newly   tamed
as if there might have been   something wrong
with me   and now   I was fixed

WHITE BIRDS

At three, I stepped on Dad's liquor
bottle and now there's a robin's
nest, faint and white, on the inside
of my left foot. It never went away.
Sometimes, when I'm silent I can hear
our old neighbor's Ford like yesterday
isn't another country, like yesterday
couldn't toss me a beautiful lifetime
so I could ruin it. A body is a sticker
book, a child's introduction to memory.
My collection, my prized white birds —
if sold at auction, might save the world.

THIS IS ALL I KNOW ABOUT HAVING A HEART

It never happens twice,
      the beluga blows,
the sun hangs grey and washed
      like an old comforter
on a grandmother's clothesline.
      We are quickly fucked
under a sunset, like lace in an oven.
      To have a heart
is to have a task, to have a heart
      I know, sounds
like gravity had a baby,
      but it didn't— it's just
floating on the first rib
      the original error of life.

EYELASHES

Unruly like wild snakes, like Satan's
pubic hairs. The gates to hell.

The door to a swamp —
toad-green and fermenting.

My father's eyelashes, a thousand
mini-machetes.

His corkscrew eyelashes, his rabid
eyelashes, his scorpion eyelashes.

My father's eyelashes — the first
fluttering thing I wanted to bury.

RENOVATING A HOUSE WHILE DRUNK

after Lynn Emmanuel

This morning I'm thinking about the closet
my father built for me with his bare hands
while drunk on Forty Creek because I love
to be sad before lunch. Go away,
he said when my mother found him
crying on the closet floor,
two feet sticking out the door
like cattle ready for market.
I'm thinking about how
my bedroom had a lock
on the door, how my father
had to fix the kitchen builder's mistakes
then slept in the bathtub
for the evening. The sound of the faucet,
like heavy rain on red ankles. We children
sat with our ears pressed
to the door, enjoying the music.
When I drink, I want my drunk father
back, his grey pants white at the knees
with drywall dust, eyes swirling
like milk in espresso. A man
who could fix anything.

MY FAMILY LEAVES MEXICO

because the microwave
       lighting the evening
crept into my metaphor
       without asking
if I wanted to see.
       Because after dinner
we laid in the rusty
       pick-up like tranquillized
cattle and no one came
       to turn on the stars.
Because I ran
       out of alliteration
after fleeing and freeing
       tied my tongue.

FATHER LEADS MARRIAGE COUNSELLING IN OUR LIVING ROOM

1.
I won't lie.
I went to the spa today
because it snowed in April
and I'd love to make it
till May.

Fog hovered over the hot tub
like exhaust exhaling
from an angel's Corvette. I chose lilac
for my fingers and toes
this month. There were wool blankets
in the sauna and no wonder —
we're all going to die
the same way. Little buds
on branches. Slow dynamite.

2.
A pink patch of rock
sits on the Elora Gorge
like a salmon who flew
and only made it halfway
to heaven. In water,
my fingers crimp
into chiffon layers —

for a moment I visit
mermaid world
before God whips me
back to Earth,
measures me out
like a cake slice and
curses me with a desire
to walk.

3.
How does a hawk know when to stop
flapping and when to start
soaring? I could tell you
a sad story that would
make you think
about the question
differently. But I don't want
to make you cry
before breakfast. Father would say
it's impolite. A safe
rebellion. A poem.
It's the way I have survived.

4.
Father leads marriage counselling
in our living room every Friday night.
I remember weeping
when the hutch wouldn't fit
through the doorway and Mother's
hands weren't Velcro, she let them slip.

I still remember how Father opened
his chest, letting a thousand hornets loose
on Mother. Some crawled
through his throat. They had red
eyes — electric cherries.

5.
Three couples sat on the couch
that night. Father anointed them.
Mother wore long sleeves.

DEAR SISTER, I'M SORRY

I found your body limp
like tulips
        when I couldn't tame
        the bucking earth
for you. I am sorry for Father's scream,
        as sharp as a dry corn husk —
        it must
        have woken you. I watched
                your eyelids retreat
like low tide,
        each white ball a sorry
moon.

YOU MIGHT HAVE TO RUN FOR A HUNDRED MILES IN THE DESERT

Four women in my family know the recipe
for continuing. It is this way: The treadmill heart

wins in the end. I promise, love. How you surrendered
is not a mystery. Or a miracle. Knees like potholes,

hips like that broken Ford in first gear. No,
you remember the silk spit in your mouth,

thick and tart from fleeing. The border guards and their fish
and fur hands. There is no pretty way to save yourself.

LOVE DOES NOT EXIST

except in the black licorice
lake, two ships splashing
like children. But then love
does not exist when one
stops. I'm from a family
where it hurts to cough
out loud. Not in the lungs,
but in the medical belly
of a soul. Where two forceps
pull dreams from our scalps
for fun. What are we waiting
for then, except to die?

II.

"I am rooted, but I flow."

—Virginia Woolf

INNER CHILD

As my grandfather once said:
If you wear gloves
you can touch anything.
My hands are hot
inside the orange
mittens — I juggle
the hurt of the world,
sharp like a single fish
scale, and the dream
of being whole,
now tinged like boiled
mulberries.

I am just pretending
to have fun
but I actually hate it
when my two hands
grow into wooden bridges,
bronze like dark beer,
and a child tries to cross
in the middle of the night
but I'm sleeping.

THE FOREPLAY OF LEAVING

I almost fell through the hole
in your truck bed the summer
you taught me how to fly
fish — it's a miracle: any mouth
waiting to be fed. The desire
to get away with survival.
We all must surrender to it.
Eventually, I got bored with tricking
fish and suggested a picnic break. Wait
here, you said and pushed my knees apart
and bit the inside of my thighs
like we were a beginning
and you never thought I'd finish.

SOFT BOYS

Our next-door neighbor Brian drives a freshly divorced
Honda Accord and every morning it mouth breathes
into the frigid air before he leaves. We don't know
if he's single or just lonely or if he works at the library
or the University in the town ten minutes over
or why a woman with knives for eyebrows
drives by every night at six and then leaves at seven
with a stack of dirty Tupperware in her hands.
When I was thirteen, a boy sat with me
in stillness and I've never been the same.
Nobody talks about how all the soft boys
saved the girls with fucked-up fathers.
The summer before high school, he pulled
my hair back like two rabbits' ears,
and as he leaned in to kiss me,
I let his freckles flutter onto my face — the salt
of the entire earth.

FARMING

Light-blue night   sky like   washed out
    jeans from five   years ago
ending with you   know what let's open
      our pants   in front of the honey
crisp section   of the orchard   behind the tractor
   shed   a hand finds warmth   easily
survival   or sense   is there a difference

   I said no blurry lines   we're getting married
after this   a truth we bit between teeth
     a gag   a silencer   a prayer
do you remember   how you stole
  the turquoise sky and slipped it
between my thighs   fed me the word *yes*
  and I lapped July air   to stay there
with you   I ripped the grass
   with my toes   and the earth yelped —

I HOLD ONTO YOU LIKE AN EGG IN A RAINSTORM

I blossom my umbrella and run —
quick! I won't get you wet! I say this
when I don't know how to love you yet.

Rain skates across my face — the sky's
careless slap. I trip and you're dry,
and you're broken.

I REMEMBER EVERYTHING

by a Loretta. Or a Taylor
or a Reba. All we had
were tapes in the forest
green minivan. At sixteen,
I fell in love in rubber boots
with chicken shit
on the soles and perhaps
I could have bartered
in the outlet section
for a real man. But my old man
was mean and there was no time,
so I belted my heart
to the first waist I could find.

RATS AND STARS

My mother used to turn leftovers
into a whole new dish with just lard
and a little flour. Some things,
when rearranged, just work themselves out.

Years ago, I heard a woman lost herself
in a cornfield for thirty days,
stayed full on rats and stars.
What saved her in the end was the light

reflecting off her collarbones, seen from miles
above. Eventually, we attract
what's good. It's possible, I'm arguing,
to stay alive on very little.

I'M TRYING TO UNDERSTAND

how a weeping willow sways so low
to the ground, never fully spilling
its salty tears. How a dancing human
becomes grey then food
for maggots. I do not know
how time zones work, how bread grows
with bacteria, or how in the summer
before seventh grade, my body morphed
into a lighthouse. I am perplexed
by the color blue and endings.
In Mexico City, I question the water
and the cab drivers. I wonder how these crimes
are different from my own sins—how a city
can resemble a church,
and how a church is never not a person.

HOW TO WRITE A SYMPATHY CARD

I'm under the moon
for you. I hate this
bony, itchy life — fucked
as a fallen feather —
for you. I'm thoroughly
unimpressed, devotedly
pissed and breaking
like a forced breath
for you.

NAMING CEREMONY

Lovely light it is, the water said
to the lighthouse. Scent of trillium

and fresh tattoos fill the air. The keeper
sinks his knees into the dark corduroy

of his job. Over and over and over
again — the knees will memorize the dip.

My knees remember bowing like old daffodils,
tricking a thousand men into naming me:

wanted.

THINGS THAT COULD BE A MOON

1. The sclera of an eyeball
2. Two women spooning
3. Dad uncurling his fist
4. Boiled potatoes
5. Any grandmother praying
6. The dip of a snow tiger's back
7. A smile like a slingshot

SMALL HURTS

A squished loaf of French bread
at the bottom of the grocery
bag. A stripped faucet
handle. That white skirt I wore
the night I became a woman,
the way it whimpered
like a red bird, eager to escape
a nest. How my voice cracked
like dry pasta when you told
me the earrings were silver,
not gold. A good poem without
a title. Pineapple. Parking
spots you have to back out
of. The color red. Opening
your eyes when there's light.

A SHEPHERD AND A DEAD BIRD

Years ago, we found a baby bird with cartoon eyes and a scarf
of feathers wrapped around its bleeding neck. Its feet skittered
like wild marbles. My sister made a cardboard box bed
with an old dishcloth for a pillow. We closed the lid tight
before going to school. If a shepherd loses even one sheep,
he will leave the rest and go search the globe. No wonder
the world is so lonely. Everyone is trying to make sense
of their tragedies, while God has been busy chasing me
through green puddles for a decade. Lucky me. Listen,
this is not a work of art, it's a command. Someone call
the shepherd and tell him I'm stuck inside a damn
good poem. The lid is sealed shut. Lord, let me out.

BECAUSE I DON'T HAVE SPOTIFY PREMIUM

I listen to Hozier on YouTube, let the next song play, and the next
one after that, and it eventually always starts playing The Fray. All of
a sudden it's bedtime, I'm in a lace baby doll top, drinking wine that
warms my throat, writing poems about flirting with God (which is
really just living — there's no difference) and *you found me, you
found me lyin' on the floor surrounded* starts playing. It takes one
verse until I remember what it feels like to worship, to fly so close to
Him our chests bump midair. To feel like the entire church might
bleed out if my sternum doesn't get it together. For one song, God
and I, we're together again, cutting up the dance floor of my soul.
We sway until my feet are bloody, until a Coldplay song comes on
and saves me.

III.

DEATH IN 2056

I used to know the way back home
after a bad storm. Now, I am unaware.
I am spooled. The road behind our farm
that led to the creek we caught crayfish in
pooled so quickly we had to drive the illegal
Ford in first gear up the gravel laneway.
Even a bad truck got us home. Which is to say
my father died. I am thinking in muscle
memory—is there any other way? Will the road
to heaven become muddy? Is it my fault? I can't stop
crying. I am ruining my Paradise.

I'M NOT THE GIRL

who loves the sun
so much she snaps
        every time the red turns
                real like vodka
hiding in a house
        where father beats
                holes into dreams

        there's a lot of good in my apartment:
                an oil painting of two pears
                three bags of backup rice
                a side table that smells
                like sex

even though I'm a girl
        with a bed
                in the kitchen

you must think I'm poor

        but he still wanted me

on the days I locked my faith
        in the laundry closet

DON'T TAKE THIS THE WRONG WAY, BUT GOD CAN'T HEAR YOU

because he has no ears
of his own. Your ears are his.
You think there is space between
the two of you—a whole sky,
fat as a blue whale—
but there isn't! God can't even see you
in your Doc Martens and red cashmere
scarf from the consignment store.
There is no celestial *and* woman.
In fact, all 3.95 billion gods
wake up every morning
in little apartments, get dressed
in colours that can scream, and roam
the world in boots just like yours.

THE DAY AFTER YOU DECIDE TO KEEP LIVING,
I LEARN

apparently, you can bite off your finger
as easily as a baby carrot. Supposedly the man
upstairs had the foresight to sew shut the circuit
in your brain that lets you do it. Some impulses —
like screaming or falling asleep in a car —
you salute to. But fear or faith, as fine as dust,
stops you from crunching your own hand.
Yesterday, you were alive and today
you still are. This is all I know —
these closed circuits, like jaws, are saving us.

ANCIENT GRIEF

From now on   we cry
     like fish   there is no difference
between our tears   and the world's

Four days after they split   the Red Sea
    it went back to being a bitch
and breathless   it had no shame

RELAPSE

For a while, I thought we'd find Jesus
again and quit our day jobs
and drinking and walk to Mexico
in seventeen weeks. Maybe scribble
about it in a diary that Penguin
picks up for a little cash. And you
know, I imagined we'd risk forever
like you do taking home a stray
dog. Even if it's not a good one,
you keep it. Though it's been a while,
you remember how to feed it,
bring it water, worship it, and keep it
from dying.

RUMORS

I hear God buys solid wood
furniture for heaven's
lounges. Not the cheap shit
made of sawdust,
but real oak and maple
and mahogany, smooth
as a pelican's beak.

On Earth, the Maker
visits IKEA
and regrets his son,
the craggy cross
and all of that, even the silent
priests who idle in the expensive
lounges. They, who have no sons
of their own. They who like glass
skin and sinning.

No, I do not envy the cup of a maple
chair, the perfect cutouts
for buttocks, hollow like eyes.

SELF-DIAGNOSIS

None of my exes had a dog.
I can't watch television
alone. I am sloppy
with the weekend, never quite respecting
its luster. I prefer to get drunk
on a Tuesday. I am one tooth away
from a locked jaw at all times, one ring
away from a married woman, one accent
away from a movie career. I quit
my job this year and now instead of trembling
at the sight of my boss, I crumble
before myself. If I dare put on a Sunday
dress, my skin chews on the bones
I never picked. I am, I am, I am.

INTAKE FORM

1/ I'm not the first woman
to lose a father
to memory.

2 / When I get bored
           of writing about spring, I sing
Garth Brooks into my pillow.

3 / He taught me to work hard
at becoming needless. To say,
I'm good on my own
           like a breastplate
not: a howl, a warning shot, a sigh.

4 / Some days I want to crawl
into my throat and scrape out
           all the hymns I sang
in reverence to a God
my father custom built
           for me.

A POEM ABOUT DEATH AND TOMATOES

The plants in my garden reach
for the torso of the deck, a skeleton
of cedar.

Something dead holds
something alive — the saddest story
we can tell.

 And Father's eyes
were first romas, then oozing beefsteaks —
in ten years:
        heirlooms. Two wild,
        red things we'll never forget.

NIGHT SKY AS A TISSUE

there's a little lip
in the moon tonight
it has a cleft
like a milk
mustache
you have missed him
for three years
and he used to smile
like six o'clock —
smooth and simple
and even
as walls
like memorizing
a collar
bone
in a black
winter storm

WHAT SHOULD WE WATCH?

he asks, and I say:
the world burn, an ostrich
give birth, the reruns
of my twenty-six
years and count how many
times I almost cracked my god-
damn front teeth kissing death.

The sun, but not as a metaphor—
let's tattoo the same star
onto our pupils
until we're both baptized
in a black so dark
it almost feels right.

ENGAGED

Last week, we took my engagement ring in to get it resized so I won't lose it in the ocean, in the grey dishwater, or in my promiscuous thoughts. I hate this for my gold ring. I ask my fiancée if this isn't theft, what is? And if we get to keep the little piece they sand away (spoiler alert: they keep it). The jeweler warns us they'll have to take off more when it turns wintertime. Fingers shrink in the cold, he says. *Marriages too?* I ponder quietly, already preparing. I've never ended a relationship in the summer. It's harder to crush things when they're swollen with life like a spring robin. Too messy. My sister says sometimes when you're pregnant you can't wear your rings anymore because your fingers get so big. If you dare leave them on too long, they have to saw them off (the rings, not the fingers, sorry). I wonder if a mother remembers the day she took off her rings. Did the sun suckle on the pale lines like candy? Did the wind hurry to her hands? How must it have felt to love in contradiction? It's a wonder anyone still does it, still lets the blood run thick and red until one day you must choose: your ring or the hot blade, one millimetre from bone. Freedom or the beautiful ache of coming too close.

PLACES AN ATHEIST DOESN'T EXIST

44

in the clearance section of lululemon / god *please* a size 6 in black / in the sliver of a second between an orange and a red light / in an Uber in Mexico City / at the Uber driver's dinner table after howling for hours over horchata / between *I love you* and *I'm not in love with you* / in old creaky farmhouses / in old creaky families / nestled in the crook of his collarbone / under satin sheets / six feet buried cold and deep

IV.

"When Dolly Parton prayed over me, I believed in God again."

—*Brandi Carlile*

CHURCH PREGNANCY

It was probably growing like a fat melon
in the hospital of my mind all along. The pastor
told me a two year college nursing program
was a stumbling block to ordained marriage.
Then, my boyfriend did cocaine. And morphine.
And left me. But I was still carrying. The pregnancy
of a church is longer than nine months.
It grows in your eyeballs, in your ankles,
rots the sacral center of your wonder,
right above your belly button. The first time
you go to sleep in a house that isn't holy,
the walls are not silent. They are coaxing you
through each contraction. To be born
again is to give birth to yourself alone.

HOW ABOUT

my yellow face in the police
blue sky, stranded like a lost
star. How about daylilies
in a field of cow shit
sucking sustenance like good
gods. How about ferns
in pots as rough as a heel.
How about airplanes
and aperitif. How about I follow
you into bed with slippery
hands? How about we linger
in this hallway to hell
a bit longer? I could do this,
I could make myself obey
the earth for you.

SLOW JOY

My hymen never broke. Instead, we stretched it
over weeks. Maybe a month. So when I reached
the top, I was already desensitized to glory —
the head of the mountain was a soft skull.
But I got both: pleasure without pain.
Other people do it too: a freelance alcoholic,
Kate's husband who never got caught, a July
night without a single star. Sometimes I moonlight
a brave person just so I can feel what it's like
to wade in joy up to my hips. But it never lasts.
The moment you look at something yellow
it turns brown —

AFTERTASTE

The end of a good god lingers
like a fishbone stuck in the back
of a throat. It's impossible
to separate the meat from the bones
ahead of time — don't try. A good god leaves
a soap tray, a lint roller, and little flecks
on your navy blue sweater. She's a foolish
woman — the one who declutters,
the one who dares roll flat
all the moments of light, the edges
of the stars.

TWO CHRISTIAN GIRLS IN THE CAFÉ AGREE THAT ROMANCE BOOKS ARE PORN

Once, a horse
saddle sent me
to heaven. The dip
of the animal's back
cupped my wonder
until it pooled
like salt water,
begging me to let
go. I let go. After,
the seat reeked
of vanilla and smoke.

IT'S EASY TO FALL IN LOVE

when you're drunk on champagne
in a new city once a month.
I don't think you've loved
until you've had to lie
about the deep blue desire
to dick around with the devil. Or the lipstick
on the bottom of your sock
in the shape of a seashell, small as a fetus.
About being good.
Have you ever slurped
a soulmate — quick and sharp as an oyster?
Let the salt seep down into your wounds
until you were screaming in your sleep?

PLEASE TELL ME THERE'S A CONCLUSION TO THE OCEAN

A period or a stop made of sea urchin.
   A *no darkness past here* sign
I can steal and set up in the far
   corner of my heart. The waves
stand up urgently when I arrive
   like lonely men aroused by a good woman
who doesn't know how good
   she is. I never go further than waist
deep. The seagulls circle me: six
   guardian angels who didn't pack
a lunch. I'm hungry, too. But I stay
   alert. Swimming into an infinity
is dangerous. One toe at a time,
   I let the water swirl me
into a stupor. I give into not having
   language for leaving, no words
for what it means to party
   with a liquid grave—

DAYS WHEN I HAVE NOTHING

to do, and nothing left to cry over, I notice
the FedEx delivery driver's beard,
and how the patches lined up are an ancient
maze. I imagine his wife has written poems
about him, how she loses herself in the salt
and pepper stripes, only to find her way home
to the beaming bald spot, the crown,
of her king. Days when I'm considering
returning my birth certificate, I notice the fog
on the face of my cold office window,
and I place my hand up to it. Each finger
finds a spot. A labyrinth — no, a template —
for continuing.

SOUND BATH FOR RE-ANOINTING

First, the pre-chorus of "Everglow"
by Coldplay. Then blood oranges —
the alto rip of a peel. Try slapping
canoe paddles and breaking beer
bottles. Then, December's moan, soft
like cut marshmallows. It's okay to crave
a wasted whisper, but after a week, move on
to the whine of a dishwasher. It has a beggar's
breath, but it's something you can love.

THE ONE WHERE I FORGET TO BE SAD ON INSTAGRAM WHILE THE COUNTRY BENEATH ME CRUMBLES

The thing is, I need to cut my hair
short like Frida after she ditched
Diego, except I need love like lice
needs a thousand strands of gold
to sleep at night. So I have a problem.
I want to sing heartbreak poems
into the mouth of my man, my perfect
man. Love is a better way. To write
death. Maybe, I think. All neck-deep
in living. Squash blossoms in my garden
and the world is folding into itself
like a selfish paper plane. I want two kids
and a mansion. I want to not remember
the word *burning*.

THE BEGINNING OF IT ALL

Maple leaves in the backyard
        like leather shavings.
The garden molds
        from the edges.

Sighs. Sits
on the edge of August like she's a bathtub —

                shhhhhh.

                The magic manifests
at night — the sweaters are knit
from umbilical cords, feeding
the strangeness
                between seasons.

THERE IS NO ALGORITHM TO PREDICT DIVORCE

from a deity. Or a lover, or a house
disguised as a family. The for-you-page
of the rest of your life isn't in your control.
Your ancestors fucked you over
a long time ago. So laugh a little,
make love before marrying, and worship
tomatoes, silkworms, wet dirt—
anything that makes you weep.

V.

“I was a late bloomer. But anyone who blooms at all, ever, is very
lucky.”

—*Sharon Olds*

I THINK I PULLED A LITTLE GOD FROM MY MOUTH

is what she said
the night they found
her throat in the alleyway
behind HomeSense, rolling
around in vernix
and blood. No time
to call the doctor,
her jaw had simply hinged
open like a red tulip
on autopilot in April.
Rumor has it
this woman birthed
a voice the size of her life.

OLD LOVERS

It's our fiftieth anniversary, well on our way to dying.
The day has turquoised, the porch is swept,
and we're parched for each other like gravlax.
We sip lemon-green tea on the swing and play a game
of *remember when*. Maybe this is perfection,
and perfect doesn't mean forever, after all. So I fumble
for your buckle and I take you — familiar like a house —
between both hands, and I shiver you for the thousandth
time. You unbutton my cardigan like a pianist,
and I show you myself, speckled as wild cod, breasts soft
like two hammocks. We sway like this, the wind
of our whole lives pushing us onwards.

IN THE MORNING, WE ARE SHIPS

Sorry, I mean we sleep
beside each other in the hell
of morning, mouths sloppily
closed. Your eyelashes, yolked
over, buzz like little beasts, as if to wake
you gently. The freckles in the hull
of your face swim to the surface.
What feels more like waking up
drenched in together,
than moving this ship, one oar each,
back to the yellow shore?

DEAR COREY

after Ocean Vuong's "Dear Peter"

I wish it were simple
       for you to love me
all the time but
       every month there's a week
where I have a fillet knife
       for a body and hands
like a mean mother you
       know how I get
all brown in my mind when my belly
       spills over my jeans
and women promised me
       I'm still beautiful
oh well it's on purpose probably
       how soft
rhymes with offed I suppose
       I'm over-
whelmed when something
       is two things
at once like salted caramel
       and a sad, kind person

SOMEWHERE, A PACIFIER IS USED

for the last time. A child lets go.

Dusk groans as I fall asleep
on his pullout couch. A grandma

puts her oxygen aside. Time
is passed around like diamonds

in a good family. We borrow
each other's last closed fists.

MY DOCTOR SAYS HAVING A BABY WILL CURE MY ENDOMETRIOSIS

"In a dream, you are never eighty." —Anne Sexton

So I am still
standing here
in a linen dress,
fresh and flat
as a green onion,
crying for a chance
to grow a throat,
a perfect heart,
two little legs, soft
like warm potatoes.

TONIGHT   I AM TRYING   TO OPEN UP

my sacral chakra   with carnelian   and pigeon
pose   and affirmations   like

I invite pleasure   into all areas   of my life

I want to ask   my naturopath who closed
this cave   who crested   the top of my pubic
bone   like a whale   the spot
right above   my belly
button   who dared   venture
between   my sternum and my wonder

who pitched   a tent   danced with fire
for feet   and who   before remembering
to leave   fell asleep.

EASILY

I could have become a woman
who needs to slurp at the nape
of a brown bottle
to feel something. Easily,
I could have visited Oaxaca
and thought about tying
the orange sky, wet like a silk scarf,
around my neck. Easily, I could have lipped
one too many bar boys and ended up with two
strollers and a court date. But I didn't.
Every morning, I wake my poems
and we nuzzle like small horses.
The clouds are purple. I'm truly alone.

LOVE LEAVES LEFTOVERS

It's been three years and I still have the French
keyboard enabled on my phone. Occasionally,
when I comment on poems on the internet,
it autocorrects *love* to *liberté*.
It's been three years and I still sleep
facing the window because it's *good*
to feel the sun when you wake. Every time
I see a squirrel, I think of how you, utterly amazed
by their existence, tried to feed them peanuts
off your balcony railing. And how they came
to you and gently nuzzled your hands. I've never shit-
talked squirrels since. Love leaves leftovers, I've
learned. It's never a clean escape. Oh, but what a way
to say goodbye: *Here, I've loved you, save some for later.*

THINGS I'VE MEMORIZED TRYING TO STAY ALIVE

The menu at Bar George in Montréal, everything —
the apps, the cocktails, and even the wines,
how the Cabernet Franc is alphabetized
incorrectly. How to count money
like regrets. Five ways to escape
in high heels. How to fly fast without looking
like you're running. The airport
code to every gorgeous city. Why flamingos
become pink. How to please. How to glow
in the dark. The curve of a Maserati's
back seat, a ramp to a good life,
the charred cost of a future.

MEDIUM

Observed from many miles away,
the billboard on the way to my yoga
studio faintly resembles two nipples

and a head of black hair. *Past, present, future,*
it reads from close up. I'm not sure
what to make of this marketing

genius, except that I've memorized
her phone number,
and I might not need a god after all.

I STILL WANT TO BE A GOOD PERSON

even though I am a June bug
without a father. Even though the grass is brown
and it's all my fault. Even though the dead
speak to me and I gatekeep their wisdom. Ha.
Bold hair on someone's arms — let me return
as fear. I want to be a good person
even though I lasso my neck towards death,
dip my finger into the sunset before my elders
have eaten. I am a jar of marmalade. I am a lid.
I am a fool with a tight grip. There's nothing left
except for me. For me.

RECLAIM

It's been forever since Mom had a straight back
and Dad had a drinking problem, so today
is the kind of morning
that sits on my nose like a berry
cardinal against the white-grey
winter air. The transport trucks
are steaming to Toronto, the neighbor's cows
are safe inside the barn, and Corey
is still sleeping soundly. Between seven
and nine, all I see is red.
Today is the day I reclaim,
I've decided. I can do this. I'll stretch
my tongue out past my nose
and eat every last rouge thing before noon.

INHERITANCE

She was sick, they will say, her whole
life rotting like autumn potatoes.

I will tell you it was a woman
who tore through drawers
like a machete to wheat.
Drained the house of hell
like a pig on a hoist in a butcher's shop.

"But it wasn't raining that night!"

They will send the samples to a lab
and find only salt — floorboards
brined in peace. In release. You are eggshell,
I will say to the walls, and gift
them a mother. I will burn the house,
walk into the back-
yard, plant my toes in the soil.

THE FINAL PREPARATION

We die with blood in our veins,
faith salivating in our mouths,
      still slick as a spring trout,
taut as a winded kite. It takes a while
for us to truly wither. This is fine,
      really, it's perfect. End comes
not like a robber at midnight,
but like a stray cat to a front door,
      tamed over weeks. One must trust
the recipe for dying, perhaps even prepare
a little by slipping a finger
      into the Reaper's jaw.
Let the salt be sucked off, easy
like a rib. Let it fall off the bone.

CREDITS

Thank you to the editors of the following journals in which these poems first appeared, sometimes in earlier versions.

Narrative: "White Birds"

The Literary Review of Canada: "Night sky as a tissue" & "Dear sister, I'm sorry"

Only Poems: "How About," "I Think I Pulled A Little God From My Mouth," "This Is All I Know About Having A Heart," "Don't Take This The Wrong Way But God Can't Hear You," "Somewhere, A Pacifier Is Used," & "A Little Feral"

Contemporary Verse 2: "Medium" & "Places An Atheist Doesn't Exist"

Queen's Quarterly: "My Father, A Horse Whisperer" & "Renovating A House While Drunk"

Gyroscope Review: "Love Leaves Leftovers"

The Wild Umbrella: "Old Lovers" & "Self-Diagnosis"

San Pedro River Review: "The One Where I Forget To Be Sad On Instagram While The Country Beneath Me Crumbles."

Falling Leaf Journal: "Because I Don't Have Spotify Premium"

Pinhole Poetry: "Things I've Memorized Trying To Stay Alive"

The Temz Review: "Easily"

Grain: "I Still Want To Be A Good Person"

North Meridian Review: "In The Morning, We Are Ships"

The Chestnut Review: "A Poem About Death And Tomatoes"

"Eyelashes" is inspired by Dion O'Reilly's poem "My Mother's Hands."

"You Might Have To Run For A Hundred Miles In The Desert" is inspired by a line from Mary Oliver's poem "Wild Geese." Oliver's line is "you do not have to walk on your knees for a hundred miles in the desert."

An earlier version of the poem "Inner Child" was originally published in *longcon magazine* and is inspired by the painting "Bar Boy" by Salman Toor (2019).

"Dear Corey" is after Ocean Vuong's poem "Dear Peter."

The title of "Renovating A House While Drunk" is after Lynn Emmanuel's poem "Frying Trout While Drunk."

The structure of "My Family Leaves Mexico" was inspired by Ocean Vuong's poem "Essay On Craft."

Samfifty four literary magazine: "Please Tell Me There's A Conclusion To The Ocean"

ACKNOWLEDGEMENTS

To Derrick, Haley, and the entire Write Bloody team. I'm beyond grateful for your expertise, your dedication, and care. Thank you.

To Alison Pick, for your life changing mentorship. I would not be here without you.

To Isabelle Correa first and foremost for your friendship, but also for bolstering earlier versions of this manuscript with honest care.

To every bold and gutsy writer in my writing community, *Gather.* You are my people. I know the sweetness of community because of you.

To Corey, for loving me a little feral.

ABOUT THE AUTHOR

Maria Giesbrecht is a Canadian poet whose work explores her Mexican and Mennonite roots. Her writing has appeared in *The Literary Review of Canada*, *Narrative*, *Grain*, *ONLY POEMS*, *San Pedro River Review*, and elsewhere. She is the winner of the 2025 Jack McCarthy Book Prize, the Lesley Strutt Poetry Prize, a finalist for the 2025 Narrative Poetry Prize, a Best of Net nominee, and the founder of Gather, an international writing community that connects poets worldwide. Born in Durango, Mexico, she now lives near Toronto, Canada with her fiancée.

mariagiesbrecht.com | @theguelphpoet
Photo Credit: David Casco

IF YOU LIKE MARIA GIESBRECHT, MARIA LIKES....

Good Girl and Other Yearnings by Isabelle Correa
Morphology by Erica Miriam Fabri
Let Go With the Lights On by Lexi Pelle
Wailing on Whisper Street by Bree Bailey
Help in the Dark Season by Jacqueline Suskin

Write Bloody Publishing publishes and promotes great books of poetry every year. We believe that poetry can change the world for the better. We are an independent press dedicated to quality literature and book design, with an office in Los Angeles.

We are grassroots, DIY, get it done believers. Pull up a good book and join the family.

Support independent authors, artists, and presses

**Want to know more about Write Bloody books, authors and events?
Join our mailing list at**

www.writebloody.com

WRITE BLOODY BOOKS

After the Witch Hunt — Megan Falley

Against Vanishing — Cristin O'Keefe Aptowicz

Aim for the Head: An Anthology of Zombie Poetry — Rob Sturma, Editor

Allow The Light: The Lost Poems of Jack McCarthy — Jessica Lohafer, Editor

Amulet — Jason Bayani

Any Psalm You Want — Khary Jackson

Atrophy — Jackson Burgess

Birthday Girl with Possum — Brendan Constantine

The Bones Below — Sierra DeMulder

Born in the Year of the Butterfly Knife — Derrick C. Brown

Bouquet of Red Flags — Taylor Mali

Bring Down the Chandeliers — Tara Hardy

Broke Stay Broke — Tim Stafford

Built By Storms —Miriam Kramer

Ceremony for the Choking Ghost — Karen Finneyfrock

CLAYBOY — Fez Avery

A Constellation of Half-Lives — Seema Reza

Counting Descent — Clint Smith

Courage: Daring Poems for Gutsy Girls — Karen Finneyfrock,
Mindy Nettifee, & Rachel McKibbens, Editors

Cut to Bloom — Arhm Choi Wild

Dear Future Boyfriend — Cristin O'Keefe Aptowicz

Do Not Bring Him Water — Caitlin Scarano

Don't Smell the Floss — Matty Byloos

Drive Here and Devastate Me — Megan Falley

Drunks and Other Poems of Recovery — Jack McCarthy

The Elephant Engine High Dive Revival — Derrick C. Brown, Editor

Every Little Vanishing — Sheleen McElhinney

Everyone I Love Is a Stranger to Someone — Annelyse Gelman

Everything Is Everything — Cristin O'Keefe Aptowicz

Favorite Daughter — Nancy Huang

The Feather Room — Anis Mojgani

Floating, Brilliant, Gone — Franny Choi

Glitter in the Blood: A Poet's Manifesto for Better, Braver Writing — Mindy Nettifee

Gold That Frames the Mirror — Brandon Melendez

Good Girl and Other Yearnings — Isabelle Correa

The Heart of a Comet — Pages D. Matam

Heavy Lead Birdsong — Ryler Dustin

Heirloom — Ashia Ajani

Here I Am Burn Me — Kimberly Nguyen

Her Whole Bright Life — Courtney LeBlanc

Hello. It Doesn't Matter. — Derrick C. Brown

Help in the Dark Season — Jacqueline Suskin

Hot Teen Slut — Cristin O'Keefe Aptowicz

How the Body Works the Dark — Derrick C. Brown

How to Love the Empty Air — Cristin O'Keefe Aptowicz

I Love Science! — Shanny Jean Maney

I Love You Is Back — Derrick C. Brown

I Now Pronounce You — Caroline Earleywine

The Importance of Being Ernest — Ernest Cline

The Incredible Sestina Anthology — Daniel Nester, Editor

In Search of Midnight — Mike McGee

In the Pockets of Small Gods — Anis Mojgani

Junkyard Ghost Revival — Derrick C. Brown, Editor

Keep Your Little Lights Alive —John-Francis Quiñonez

Kissing Oscar Wilde — Jade Sylvan

The Last American Valentine — Derrick C. Brown, Editor

The Last Time as We Are — Taylor Mali

Learn Then Burn — Tim Stafford & Derrick C. Brown, Editors

Learn Then Burn Teacher's Guide — Tim Stafford & Molly Meacham, Editors

Learn Then Burn 2: This Time It's Personal — Tim Stafford, Editor